0

zero

zero

10

ten

dieci

20

twenty

venti

30

thirty

trenta

40
forty

quaranta

50
fifty

cinquanta

60
sixty

sessanta

70
seventy

settanta

80

eigthy

ottanta

90

ninety

novanta

100

one hundred

cento

1000

one thousand

mille

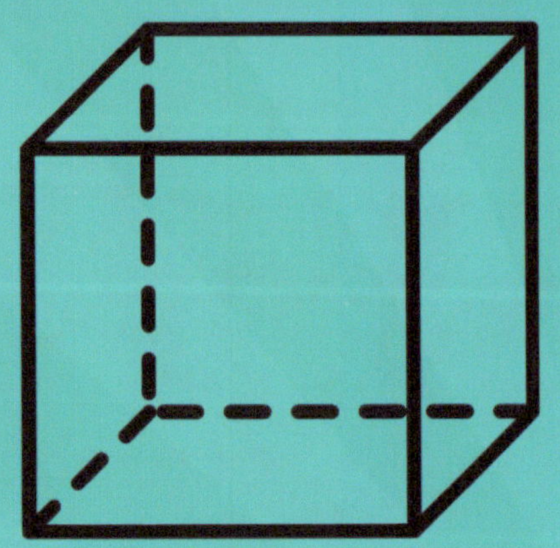

cube

cubo

block

blocco

ice cube

cubetto di ghiaccio

caramel

caramello

sugar

zucchero

dice

dadi

gift box

confezione regalo

cardboard box

scatola di cartone

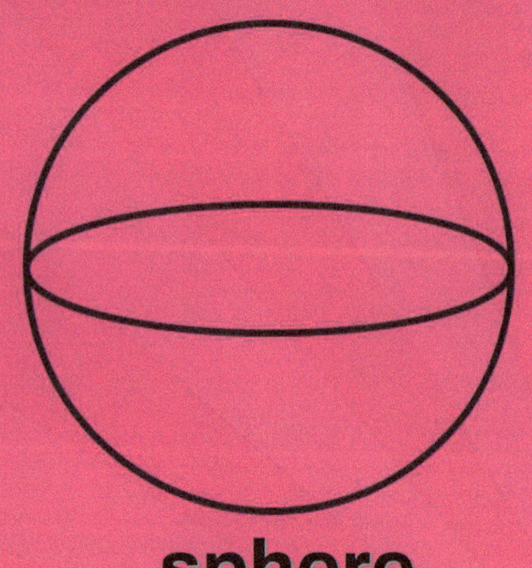

sphere

sfera

ice cream scoop

pallina di gelato

pearl

perla

bubble

bolla

marbles

biglie

planet

pianeta

snowball

palla di neve

tennis ball

pallina da tennis

cylinder

cilindro

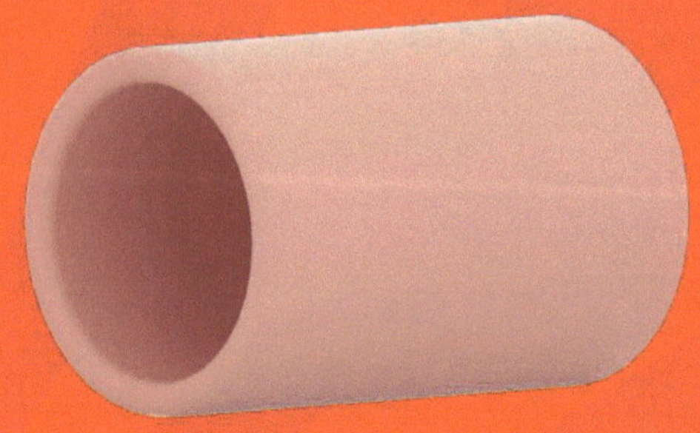

tube

tubo

batteries

batterie

thread spool

rocchetto di filo

cinnamon

cannella

rolling pin

mattarello

sausage

salsiccia

hay bale

balla di fieno

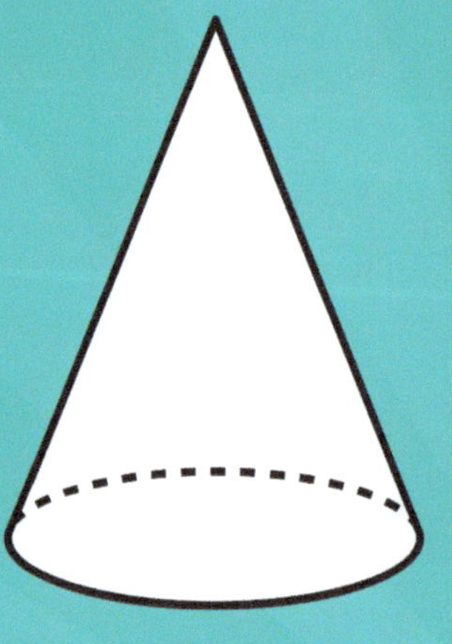

cone

cono

road cone

cono stradale

ice cream cone

cono gelato

witch hat

cappello da strega

dungeon

maschio di castello

fir tree

abete

party hat

cappello da festa

snail

lumaca

blackberry

mora

currant

ribes

clementine

clementina

durian

durian

dragon fruit

frutto del drago

jackfruit

giaco

star fruit

carambola

asparagus

asparago

radish

ravanello

red bean

fagiolo rosso

turnip

rapa

cassava

manioca

sweet potato

patata dolce

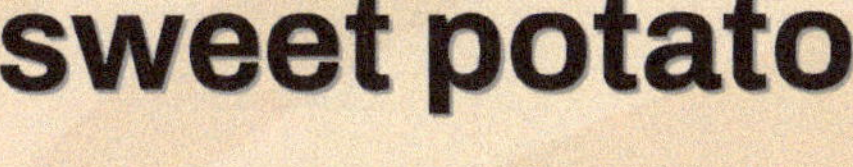

chickpeas

ceci

eagle

aquila

bat

pipistrello

beaver

castoro

flamingo

fenicottero

raven

corvo

blackbird

merlo

blue tit

cinciarella

magpie

gazza

swallow bird

rondine

lark

allodola

parakeet

parrocchetto

woodpecker

picchio

peacock

pavone

parrot

pappagallo

toucan

tucano

stork

cicogna

coral

corallo

sea anemone

anemone di mare

sea urchin

riccio di mare

seahorse

cavalluccio marino

clownfish

pesce pagliaccio

goldfish

pesce rosso

crab

granchio

hermit crab

paguro

dolphin

delfino

narwhal

narvalo

octopus

polpo

squid

calamaro

whale shark

squalo balena

orca

orca

blue whale

balenottera azzurra

beluga whale

beluga

hammerhead shark

squalo martello

white shark

squalo bianco

lemon shark

squalo limone

tiger shark

squalo tigre

grasshopper

cavalletta

caterpillar

bruco

scorpion

scorpione

lizard

lucertola

dinosaurs

dinosauri

black hair

capelli neri

ginger hair

capelli rossi

brown hair

capelli castani

blond hair

capelli biondi

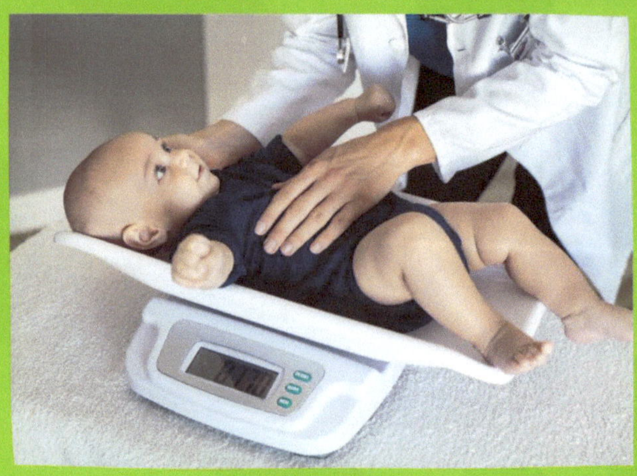

scale

bilancia

hospital

ospedale

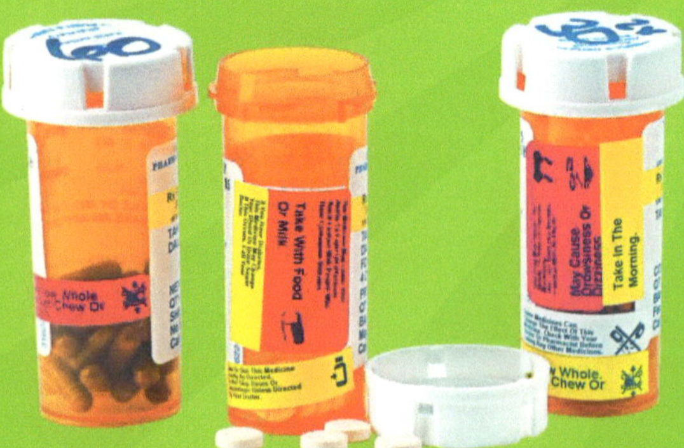

medicine

medicina

thermometer

termometro

bandage

benda

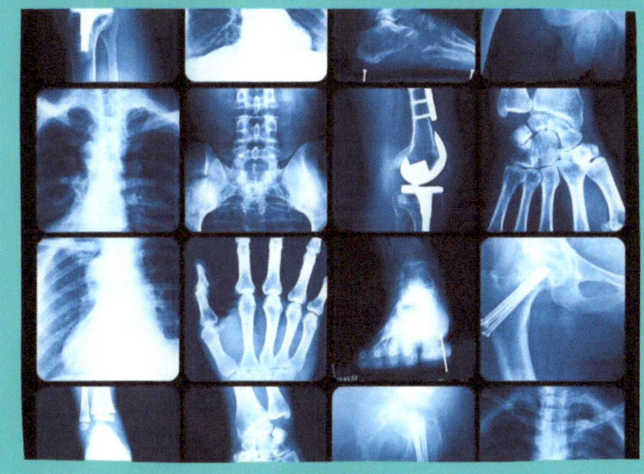

x-ray

raggi x

doctor

dottore

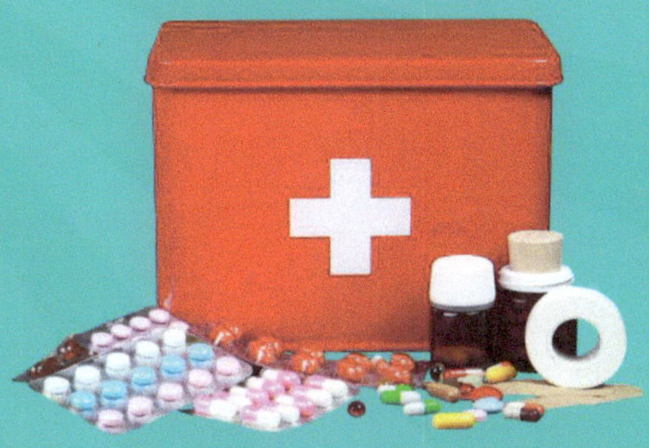

first aid kit

kit di primo soccorso

play

giocare

draw

disegnare

count

contare

write

scrivere

dancing

danza

swimming

nuoto

skiing

sci

basketball

pallacanestro

tennis

tennis

ping pong

tennis da tavolo

soccer

calcio

horse riding

equitazione

ice hockey

hockey su ghiaccio

judo

judo

boxing

pugilato

running

corsa

baseball

baseball

cricket

cricket

rugby

rugby

volleyball

pallavolo

maracas

maracas

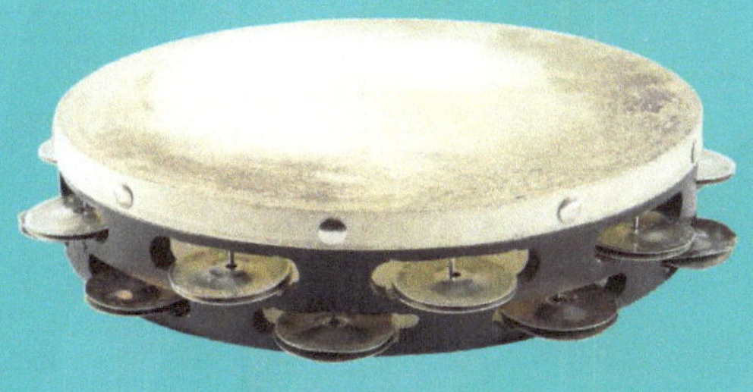

tambourine

tamburello

xylophone

xilofono

violin

violino

piano

pianoforte

guitar

chitarra

cello

violoncello

harp

arpa

drum

tamburo

djembe

djembe

drum kit

batteria

trumpet

tromba

horn

corno

saxophone

sassofono

flute

flauto

headphone

cuffie

sing

cantare

sheet music

spartiti

microphone

microfono